GW00706037

A Simple Guide to the Mass

by
Dom Cuthbert Johnson OSB

*All booklets are published thanks to the
generous support of the members of the
Catholic Truth Society*

CATHOLIC TRUTH SOCIETY
PUBLISHERS TO THE HOLY SEE

Contents

Presentation

Throughout the English-speaking world the new translation of the Latin Roman Missal, published in 2002 by Blessed Pope John Paul II, is being introduced.

This dignified and doctrinally precise text has been welcomed by the Holy Father Pope Benedict XVI who prays that it will bring about "a renewal and a deepening of Eucharistic devotion all over the English-speaking world". The Holy Father has led the way in explaining the meaning of the Liturgy as will be seen from the many quotations from his teaching and preaching that are given in this simple "Benedictine" guide to the Mass.

Preparing to Participate in the Mass

*"To prepare ourselves to celebrate the
sacred mysteries."*

Preparing to celebrate

We must prepare our minds and hearts for the celebration of Mass. "We live today in a society in which every space, every moment must be 'filled' with initiatives, activities and sound, so that there is no time for listening and dialogue. Dear brothers and sisters, don't be afraid of silence outside and inside ourselves, if we want to hear not only the voice of God but also of those who are close to us, the voices of others." (*Pope Benedict XVI*).

Unnecessary conversation both before and after the celebration of the sacred liturgy disturbs an atmosphere which is conducive to prayer and worship. Let us take to heart the poetical words of Saint John Chrysostom (347 - 407): "the church is the dwelling of angels; it is the kingdom of God; it is heaven itself so in the church let only spiritual things be spoken."

As we enter the church and pass through the door let us recall the words of the Lord: "I am the door" (John 10:9). We bless ourselves with Holy Water as a reminder "of the sacrament of baptism, through which we become

sharers in the death and resurrection of Jesus Christ."
(*Pope Benedict XVI*)

Through our genuflection to the Blessed Sacrament we acknowledge that have come into the presence of the Lord and proclaim our faith in the real presence. We then take our place as members of "a chosen race, a royal priesthood, a holy nation" and prepare ourselves to celebrate the sacred mysteries.

Behaviour

"*Let us consider how we ought to behave in the presence of God.*" (*Saint Benedict*).

"A liturgical celebration is always a very serious action. It must be prepared and carried out with great care in its every detail." (*Pope Paul VI*). Care for external details must be accompanied by attention to internal dispositions. To be attentive to gestures and postures makes an important contribution towards creating that atmosphere of recollection which is felt by many to be lacking in our liturgy.

Standing is a mark of respect. We stand to sing God's praises and to pray for our needs and those of all peoples on the earth. Standing is also a sign of waiting in readiness for the Lord. To stand up is to give witness and make an affirmation; that is why we stand to profess our faith.

Kneeling is a sign of penitence and a gesture of supplication. It is a powerful symbol of adoration and of acknowledgement of our dependence upon the Lord our God, Creator of heaven and earth. It is a gesture which we find frequently in Scripture and it has an important place in the Liturgy.

The profound bow is a deep sign of reverence. A profound bow is made when passing in front of the altar and during the Creed. The bowing of the head is a sign of reverence.

Sitting is a position for listening and learning, just as Mary of Bethany sat at the Lord's feet and listened to his teaching. We sit to listen to the word of God and to ponder it in our hearts in prayer.

When we walk in procession we are reminded that we are the pilgrim people of God.

The House of the Lord

Where Christians gather to celebrate the sacred mysteries are found the altar, ambo and the chair of the one who presides at the assembly.

The Altar

The altar is the place on which the sacrifice of the Cross is made present and it is the holy table of the Lord to which we have been invited.

Enough emphasis has not been laid upon the holiness and sacred character of the altar. To the altar we bring ourselves, our offerings and prayers of petition, praise and thanksgiving. Devotion to the altar is founded upon the mystery which is celebrated there: "May this altar be the place where the great mysteries of redemption are accomplished: a place where your people offer their gifts, unfold their good intentions, pour out their prayers, and echo every meaning of their faith and devotion." (*Prayer from Rite of the Dedication of an Altar*).

The Ambo

The place from which the Word of God is proclaimed is called by the Fathers of the Church "a throne for the word of God and the seat of wisdom". It is by hearing the word and sharing in the bread of life that we grow into the full stature of Christ.

The Chair

The Eucharist is the action of Christ and the people of God hierarchically assembled. The president's chair is a sign of his ministry of service in imitation of the Lord who came not to be served but to serve and give himself for us.

The Structure of the Mass

"We must learn to understand the structure of the liturgy and why it is laid out as it is." (*Pope Benedict XVI*)

The essential elements in the structure of the Mass have remained unchanged from the time of the Apostles. There have been developments and enrichments in the form of the Mass but as Pope Benedict remarked: "The liturgy which developed in the course of two millenniums has always remained a continuation of ongoing growth of worship and proclamation."

There are two parts in the Mass that make up one single act of worship: the liturgy of the Word and the liturgy of the Eucharist.

The Liturgy of the Word is made up of the proclamation of readings from Holy Scripture, the homily, the Creed, (on Sundays and Solemnities) and ends with the Bidding Prayers.

The Liturgy of the Eucharist begins with the procession and presentation of the bread and wine for the holy sacrifice. When the prayer over the Gifts has been said the celebrant begins the Eucharistic Prayer. After the Great Amen at the end of the Eucharistic Prayer the preparation for Holy Communion begins with the Our

Father and the prayer for the peace and unity of the Church. While the hymn Lamb of God is sung, there takes place the ancient and sacred gesture of the "breaking of the bread". After Communion and thanksgiving the liturgy of the Eucharist is brought to a close with the prayer after Communion.

As is fitting, these two parts of the Mass, Word and Sacrament, are preceded by an introduction and followed by a conclusion.

The introductory rites are: the entrance chant and the veneration of the altar, followed by the greeting, the Act of Penance, the Lord have mercy, the Glory to God (when prescribed), and the Collect Prayer which concludes the introductory rites.

The Mass ends with the concluding rites which consist of the final greeting and blessing, followed by the dismissal, the veneration of the altar and the out-going procession.

Once we have grasped the structure of the Liturgy and its various parts we must make it our own. "We must interiorize the structure, the words of the liturgy, the Word of God. By doing this, our celebration truly becomes a celebration "with" the Church. Our hearts are enlarged and we are not doing just anything but are "with" the Church, in conversation with God." (*Pope Benedict XVI*).

The Introductory Rites

"Where two or three are gathered in my name, there am I in the midst of them." (Matthew 18:20)

The Introductory Rites help the congregation to become "one mind and heart", ready to listen attentively to the proclamation of the word of God and to participate in celebration of the holy Eucharist.

Entrance Chant

The entrance chant accompanies the procession of the Celebrant and ministers to the altar and helps to introduce the assembly to the season, Feast or mystery that is being celebrated.

Veneration of the Altar and Greeting of the People

As the Celebrant and the ministers reach the place of celebration, they make a sign of honour and reverence to Blessed Sacrament and to the altar. The Celebrant and the ordained ministers venerate the altar with a kiss. On Sundays and Feast Days incense may be used. The Celebrant takes the censer from the Deacon or server and walks around the altar incensing it. If the Celebrant passes in front of the Cross he reverences it with incense.

The smoke rising from the censer is a symbol of the prayers of the people of God that ascend to heaven.

Sign of the Cross

"We should glory in the Cross of our Lord Jesus Christ, for He is our salvation, our life and our resurrection." (*Opening Chant for the Feast of the Exaltation of the Holy Cross*).

Our opening words and gesture are an affirmation of our baptismal profession of faith in God: Father, Son and Holy Spirit. They also remind us that we have been called to bear witness by our lives to the Gospel: "Go, therefore, and make disciples of all nations, baptizing *them in the name of the Father and of the Son and of the Holy Spirit*" (Matthew 28:19).

Amen is an ancient Hebrew word which means giving approval for what has been said or done. *Amen* is always a decisive and definitive affirmation: "so be it for it cannot be otherwise". Whenever Amen occurs in the liturgy it always has this meaning of giving assent to what has been said and accomplished.

Greeting

When the Risen Lord appeared to the disciples in the upper room He immediately greeted them: "Peace be with you". Following His example the Celebrant greets those who are assembled in the name of Christ Jesus. It is not only inappropriate to use a form of secular greeting, such as "good morning", but shows a misunderstanding of what it means to be gathered in the name of the Lord. If there is a need for a special word of welcome this must come after the greeting.

We have several forms of greeting but all are taken from holy Scripture and are among our oldest liturgical texts.

The greetings express what Saint Paul wrote to the Philippians and form a fitting preparation to our celebration. "Do not be anxious about anything, but in everything, by prayer and petition, with thanksgiving, present your requests to God. And the peace of God, which transcends all understanding, will guard your hearts and your minds in Christ Jesus."

In his greeting the Celebrant also prays that "communion of the Holy Spirit" be with us. The word communion expresses the nature of the Church. The most fundamental fellowship is not with one another, but is our communion in the life of Christ. Through the communion of the Holy Spirit we become one body, one spirit in Christ. Our fellowship in the bond of charity is the fruit of communion.

"The Church is called during her earthly pilgrimage to maintain and promote communion with the Triune God and communion among the faithful. For this purpose she possesses the word and the sacraments, particularly the

Eucharist, by which she "constantly lives and grows and in which she expresses her very nature." (*Blessed Pope John Paul II*).

The greeting "Grace to you and peace" is found in the oldest of the new Testament writings, the first Letter of Saint Paul to the Thessalonians, written about the year 55. It is wonderful that these words still find a place in our celebration of the liturgy.

The greeting "The Lord be with you" is the simplest and the most ancient of greetings. It expresses the wish that the faithful should be with the Lord and under Divine protection in order to grow into the fullness of the stature of Christ.

When the Bishop celebrates he says: "Peace be with you". This is the greeting used by the risen Lord to his disciples gathered in the upper room. These words are also a proclamation and affirmation that here in this place the mystery of the Church is made manifest.

And with your spirit

The reply of the people to all the greetings is: *And with your spirit*.

There are several expressions in the New Testament that are of Hebrew or Aramaic origin and which have remained in their original language. By continuing to use these words we retain a direct link with the beginnings of Christianity. "And with your spirit" was frequently used by Saint Paul. To the Galatians he wrote "May the grace of our Lord Jesus Christ be with your spirit" (Galatians 6: 18). With greater simplicity he greeted Timothy with the words, "the Lord be with your spirit" (2 Timothy 4: 22).

The response "And with your spirit", shows that the priest is not acting in his own name but that his ministry is from God and does not depend upon his human qualities and gifts. It reminds the priest of the great responsibility he has undertaken through ordination. The great Doctor of the Church, Saint John Chrysostom, told his congregation that by saying "and with your spirit" they were showing that they understood that the bishop celebrates the holy sacrifice, not in his own name, but in the power of the Holy Spirit.

The Act of Penitence

After the greeting the Priest invites all present to participate in a Penitential Act so that our hearts and minds may be made ready to celebrate the sacred mysteries.

To acknowledge our sin is a sign of trust in the mercy of God. Saint Cyprian in his commentary on the Lord's Prayer wrote: "When the publican prayed with the Pharisee in the temple he did not lift up his eyes boldly to heaven, nor proudly raise his hands; but beating his breast, and testifying to the sins shut up within, he implored the help of the divine mercy".

An ancient document called "The Teaching of the Apostles" written about the year 95 tells Christians: "On the Lord's day gather together, break bread and give thanks after confessing your transgressions so that your sacrifice may be pure".

We have come into the presence of the Lord giving thanks and, by acknowledging our sin, we also give thanks for his gracious love and mercy because we know that the Lord is good and forgiving and that He will grant us his gift of pardon and peace.

Through my most grievous fault

In holy Scripture striking one's breast is a way of showing profound sorrow for having offended God. The repetition of "through my fault" is meant to convey the sincerity of the words expressing repentance.

Signs and symbols are an integral part of the Liturgy and therefore body language, such as striking the breast, standing, kneeling and bowing have a significant place in our celebrations.

After each of the various forms of the Penitential Act the celebrant invokes the mercy of God so that with our sins forgiven we may be admitted to the heavenly kingdom.

Lord, have mercy

With these words the faithful acclaim the Lord is God and implore His mercy. This ancient prayer was introduced into the Roman rite at the end of the 4th century by Pope Gelasius I who died in 496.

Glory to God in the highest

This is an ancient Greek hymn with which the Church, gathered in the Holy Spirit, glorifies and praises God. The opening words are from the Gospel of Saint Luke (2:13-14) "There was with the angel a multitude of the heavenly host praising God and saying, 'Glory to God in the highest, and on earth peace to people of good will'. "This joyful hymn calls upon the faithful to celebrate the glory of God, Father, Son, and Holy Spirit: "You alone are the Most High, Jesus Christ, with the Holy Spirit, in the glory of God the Father".

"This angelic song has been recognized from the earliest days as music proceeding from God, indeed, as an invitation to join in the singing with hearts filled with joy at the fact that we are loved by God. Saint Augustine says that singing is a mark of one who loves. Thus, down the centuries, the angels' song has again and again become a song of love and joy, a song of those who love." (*Pope Benedict XVI*).

The Collect

These words, Let us pray, remind us that "Our prayer is public and common; and when we pray, we pray not for one, but for the whole people, because we the whole people are one." (*Saint Cyprian*).

The Liturgy of the Word

When the Sacred Scriptures are read to us it is God who speaks to us and through these sacred readings we are nourished at the table of God's word. The image of the two tables, the Word of God and the Eucharist, is found in the teaching of the great Fathers of the Church. "From the table of the Lord we receive the bread of life... And from the table of Sunday readings we are nourished with the doctrine of the Lord." (*Saint Augustine*).

"There are two tables in the treasures of the Church. One is the table of the holy altar on which rests a consecrated bread, the precious body of Jesus Christ. The other is the table of the divine Law." (*The Imitation of Christ*).

The Word of the Lord

After each reading the assembled people by their acclamation "Thanks be to God" show that they have heard and welcomed the Word of God in faith and with gratitude.

The Responsorial psalm which follows the reading is a prayerful meditation on the word of God.

The Gospel

"We have a custom of singing Alleluia which is an old tradition of the Church: in this word is signified the praise of God" (*Saint Augustine*). Through this acclamation the faithful welcome and greet the Lord who is about to speak to them in the Gospel.

The Gospel book is carried in procession to the place of its proclamation, accompanied by candles and incense. Such marks of reverence help to prepare the minds and hearts of all present as they stand to listen to the holy reading.

"When the Gospel is to be read at Mass, stand up to show that you are ready and equipped to walk on the way that the Gospel commands." (*Saint Francis de Sales*).

Glory to you, O Lord

"Let us therefore hear the Gospel just as if we were listening to the Lord himself present" (*Saint Augustine*). We make the Sign of the Cross on our forehead, lips, and breast to expresses the desire that the words of the Holy Gospel should be in our mind, in our mouth, and in our heart.

Praise to you, Lord Jesus Christ

These words affirm our faith that through the power of the Holy Spirit, the Lord is present to us in the proclamation of the Gospel.

The Gospel is always a call to conversion, "repent and believe in the Gospel", so it is fitting that the kissing of the book be accompanied by the prayer: "Through the words of the Gospel may our sins be wiped away".

The Homily

"The homily is a means of bringing the scriptural message to life in a way that helps the faithful to realize that God's word is present and at work in their everyday lives. It should lead to an understanding of the mystery being celebrated, serve as a summons to mission, and prepare the assembly for the profession of faith, the universal prayer and the Eucharistic liturgy." (*Pope Benedict XVI*).

The Creed: Profession of Faith

The profession of faith prepares us for the celebration of the sacred mysteries. "The Creed is not a collection of propositions; it is not a theory. In the mystery of Baptism, God comes close to us and brings us closer to one another ...we say: "I believe in God the Father, the Creator of heaven and earth". We believe that at the beginning of everything is the eternal Word. With this faith we have no reason to fear. We rejoice that we can know God!" (*Pope Benedict XVI*).

The Apostles' Creed

The Apostles' Creed may be used during Lent and Easter Time.

"The Church, for her part, has given us a summary of faith in which everything essential is expressed. It is the "Apostles' Creed", which is divided into twelve articles, corresponding to the number of the twelve Apostles. It speaks of God, the creator and source of all that is, of Christ and His work of salvation, and it culminates in the resurrection of the dead and life everlasting." (*Pope Benedict XVI*).

The Prayer of the Faithful or Bidding Prayers

Saint Paul wrote to his disciple Timothy that there should be "prayers, petitions, intercessions and thanksgiving for all: for rulers and all in authority, so that we may be able to live quiet and peaceful lives in the full practice of religion and of morality" (1 Timothy 2:1-4). With these prayers the faithful exercise their baptismal priestly function, by interceding for the needs of all peoples on the earth.

The Liturgy of the Eucharist

The presentation of the gifts

"In the bread and wine that we bring to the altar, all creation is taken up by Christ the Redeemer to be transformed and presented to the Father. In this way we also bring to the altar all the pain and suffering of the world, in the certainty that everything has value in God's eyes. God invites us to participate in bringing to fulfilment his handiwork, and in so doing, gives human labour its authentic meaning, since, through the celebration of the Eucharist, it is united to the redemptive sacrifice of Christ." (*Pope Benedict XVI*).

The corporal, purificator, chalice, pall, and the Missal are placed on the altar. The faithful express their participation by making an offering and bringing forward bread and wine for the celebration of the Eucharist.

Blessed are you, Lord, God of all creation

The bread and wine are a symbol of the earth's produce and our life and work. They come to us through the goodness of God our Father from whom every good gift comes. These humble gifts, the fruit of the earth and work of human hands, will become for us the bread of life and our spiritual drink.

Wine and a little water are poured into the chalice with the words: *By the mystery of this water and wine may we come to share in the divinity of Christ who humbled himself to share in our humanity.*

The mingling of a little water with wine was the normal practice at the time of our Lord. This prayer praises God for the great mystery of the Incarnation whereby through his sharing in our human nature, Christ Jesus gave us a share in his divine nature. According to Saint Cyprian the practice of mingling water with wine was "according to the tradition of the Lord". For the holy bishop the drop of water was a sign that the Church was participating in the sacrifice of Christ. The wine represents Christ our Lord and the water the people whom he redeemed through his precious blood and washed clean in the waters of baptism.

The prayer of a "humble spirit and contrite heart" is acceptable to God (Psalm 51: 19) and so the priest prays that through our humble prayer, our sacrifice may be pleasing to the Lord our God.

Pray brothers and sisters

When the priest asks the people to pray that "my sacrifice and yours" may be acceptable we are reminded that the priest acts in the person of Christ.

The Prayer over the Offerings

Just as the Collect Prayer closes the Introductory Rites, so the Prayer over the Gifts concludes the rite of preparation. In ancient times this prayer was the only formulary used at the presentation of the gifts. These prayers ask that the gifts placed upon the altar will become for us the bread of life and pledge of eternal salvation.

The Eucharistic Prayer

"Always and for everything giving thanks in the name of our Lord Jesus Christ." (Ephesians 5: 20)

Lift up your hearts.

"The Eucharistic Prayer is the centre and summit of the entire celebration. The different Eucharistic Prayers contained in the Missal have been handed down to us by the Church's living Tradition and are noteworthy for their inexhaustible theological and spiritual richness." (*Pope Benedict XVI*).

Let us give thanks to the Lord our God.

We give thanks to the Father for the gifts of creation and His providential care. The wonders that God has done for us through His Son, Jesus Christ our Lord call for a "chorus of exultant praise". We are, therefore, invited to join our voices with the Angels and the whole heavenly host to sing the praises of God.

Holy, Holy, Holy Lord God of hosts.
Heaven and earth are full of your glory.

This hymn to the infinite holiness of God is found in the Eucharistic Prayers of both the Western and Eastern Church since the fourth century. "Holy, holy, holy is the

Lord of hosts; the whole earth is full of his glory." (Isaiah 6: 1-5). As Jesus entered Jerusalem, the crowds that went before him were shouting, "Hosanna to the Son of David! Blessed is he who comes in the name of the Lord! Hosanna in the highest!" (Matthew 21: 9).

The Eucharistic Prayer developed its form very early in the history of the Church. We can recognise it in this description given by Saint Cyril of Jerusalem (313-386). "We beg God to grant peace to all the Churches, to give harmony to the whole world, to assist all those who are in need; we all pray for all these intentions and we offer this victim for them... and last of all we pray for our deceased holy forefathers and bishops and for all those who have lived among us. For we have a deep conviction that great help will be afforded those souls for whom prayers are offered while this holy and awesome victim is present."

"From the rising of the sun to its setting, praised be the name of the Lord." (Psalm 113:3).

Make holy these gifts, we pray,
by sending down your Spirit upon them.

The Church invokes the power of the Holy Spirit that the gifts offered by human hands be consecrated, that is, become Christ's Body and Blood, and that the spotless Victim to be received in Communion, be for the salvation of those who will partake of it.

For on the night he was betrayed
he took bread, and said, "This is my Body".

"These words that Jesus spoke at the Last Supper are repeated every time that the Eucharistic Sacrifice is renewed. They lead us in spirit to the Upper Room; they make us relive the spiritual atmosphere of that night when, celebrating Easter with his followers, the Lord mystically anticipated the sacrifice that was to be consummated the following day on the Cross. The Institution of the Eucharist thus appears to us as an anticipation and acceptance, on Jesus' part, of his death. St Ephrem the Syrian writes on this topic: "during the Supper Jesus sacrificed himself; on the Cross he was sacrificed by others". (*Pope Benedict XVI*).

"The bread which we break, is it not a communion in the body of Christ? Because there is one bread, we who are many are one body, for we all partake of the one bread." (1 Corinthians 10:16-17).

He gave the chalice to his disciples, saying:
"Take this, all of you, and drink from it,
For this is the chalice of my blood".

"With these words Jesus presents himself as the true and definitive sacrifice, in which was fulfilled the expiation of sins which, in the Old Testament rites, was never fully completed. Our Lord Jesus Christ says that his

Blood 'is poured out for many' with a comprehensible reference to the songs of the Servant of God that are found in the Book of Isaiah. With the addition 'blood of the Covenant' Jesus also makes clear that through his death the prophesy of the new Covenant is fulfilled, based on the fidelity and infinite love of the Son made man. An alliance that therefore is stronger than all humanity's sins. It was during the Last Supper that he made this new Covenant with his disciples and humanity, with his own Blood, which became the 'Blood of the New Covenant'. (*Pope Benedict XVI*).

Do this in memory of me.

The Church, fulfilling the command that she received from Christ the Lord through the Apostles, keeps the memorial of Christ, recalling especially his blessed Passion, glorious Resurrection, and Ascension into heaven.

The mystery of faith.

"For as often as you eat this bread and drink the cup, you proclaim the death of the Lord until he comes." (1 Corinthians 11:26)

We celebrate the memorial of the saving Passion of your Son,
his wondrous Resurrection and Ascension into heaven,

we offer you in thanksgiving this holy and
living sacrifice.

"The prayers and rites of the Eucharistic sacrifice revive the whole history of salvation continuously before the eyes of our soul, in the course of the liturgical cycle and make us enter its significance ever more deeply." (*Saint Teresa Benedicta of the Cross*).

To us, also, your servants.

In this very memorial, the Church, gathered here, offers in the Holy Spirit the spotless Victim to the Father. The Church's intention, however, is that the faithful not only offer this spotless Victim but also learn to offer themselves, and so day by day to be consummated, through Christ the Mediator, into unity with God and with each other, so that at last God may be all in all.

For our Pope and bishop.

"The whole Catholic Church spread throughout the earth." (*Saint Polycarp*).

Prayer for the whole Church was important for the first Christian communities. Saint Polycarp shortly before his death in the year 156, prayed aloud "for all who were know to him and for the whole Catholic Church spread throughout the earth".

With all the Saints, on whose constant intercession
we rely for unfailing help.

The Eucharist is always celebrated in communion with
the entire Church, of heaven as well as of earth, and the
offering is made for her and for all her members, living
and dead, who have been called to participate in the
redemption and the salvation purchased by Christ's Body
and Blood.

Remember also our brothers and sisters
who have fallen asleep in the hope of the resurrection.

It is a holy and wholesome thought to pray for the
dead that they may be released from their sins.

"For if we have been united with him in a death like
his, we shall certainly be united with him in a resurrection
like his." (Romans 6:5)

Through him, and with him, and in him.

"For of him, and by him, and in him, are all things: to
him be glory for ever. Amen." (Romans 11: 36)

The Communion Rite

The Lord's Prayer

"The Lord's Prayer is truly the summary of the whole Gospel." (*Tertullian*).

In response to his disciples' request, "Lord, teach us to pray" (Luke 11:1), Jesus commanded them to pray the great Christian prayer, the Our Father.

"The Lord's Prayer is the most perfect of prayers... In it we ask, not only for all the things we can rightly desire, but also in the sequence that they should be desired. This prayer not only teaches us to ask for things, but also in what order we should desire them." (*Saint Thomas Aquinas*).

> For the kingdom,
> the power and the glory are yours
> now and for ever.

The acclamation "For the kingdom, the power and the glory are yours, now and forever," takes up "the first three petitions to our Father: the glorification of his name, the coming of his reign, and the power of his saving will. But these prayers are now proclaimed as adoration and thanksgiving, as in the liturgy of heaven. The ruler of this world has mendaciously attributed to himself the three titles of kingship, power, and glory. Christ, the Lord, restores them to his Father and our Father, until he hands over the kingdom to him when the mystery of salvation will be brought to its completion and God will be all in all." (*Catechism of the Catholic Church* n. 2855).

Lord Jesus Christ,
look not on our sins,
but on the faith of your Church.

"Peace I leave with you; my peace I give to you". (John 14:27). "Peace makers who sow in peace reap a harvest of righteousness." (James 4:17-18).

The sign of peace

"May the peace of the Risen Christ reign in your hearts, for as members of the one body you have been called to that peace!" (Colossians 3:15).

The altar is kissed because it has been consecrated by the invocation of the Holy Spirit. The Gospel book is kissed because through the power of the spirit Christ is present in the assembly when his word is proclaimed. The kiss of peace is given as a sign of reverence to our neighbour because, as Saint Paul tells us, our body is the temple of the Holy Spirit.

The peace of the Lord be with you always.

"It should be kept in mind that nothing is lost when the sign of peace is marked by a sobriety which preserves the proper spirit of the celebration, as, for example, when it is restricted to one's immediate neighbours." (*Sacramentum caritatis* n. 49).

The Fraction, the Breaking of the Bread

"They recognized him in the breaking of bread." (Luke 24:35).

"The 'breaking of bread' as the Eucharist was called in earliest times, has always been at the centre of the Church's life. Through it Christ makes present within time the mystery of his death and resurrection. In it he is received in person as the 'living bread come down from heaven', and with him we receive the pledge of eternal life and a foretaste of the eternal banquet of the heavenly Jerusalem." (*Blessed Pope John Paul II*).

May this mingling of the Body and Blood
of our Lord Jesus Christ
bring eternal life to us who receive it.

The mingling of the two Species is a direct preparation for the reception of the Body and Blood of the Lord and reminds us that we are destined to participate in the divinity and immortality of Christ won for us by his Passion, death and Resurrection.

Lamb of God, you take away the sins of the world,
have mercy on us.

John the Baptist looked at Jesus and pointed him out as
the "Lamb of God, who takes away the sin of the world".
By doing so, he reveals that Jesus is at the same time the
suffering Servant who silently allows himself to be led to
the slaughter and who bears the sin of the multitudes, and
also the Paschal Lamb, the symbol of Israel's redemption
at the first Passover. Christ's whole life expresses his
mission: "to serve, and to give his life as a ransom
for many".

Behold the Lamb of God, behold him who takes away
the sins of the world.

With these words John the Baptist pointed out the
Lord's Anointed when He came, and John continues his
mission to point out Christ to us until the Lord comes
again at the end of time.

Lord, I am not worthy that you should enter under my
roof, but only say the word and my soul shall
be healed.

At this most sacred moment of Communion the
Church puts on our lips, not the words of a great saint or
mystic, but those of a pagan soldier who showed great
faith and trust in the Lord and took that vital first step of
inviting him into his life. (See Matthew 8: 5-13).

Holy Communion may be received in the hand or on the tongue. Saint Cyril of Jerusalem told his congregation, "When you approach make your left hand a throne for your right hand, since the latter is to receive the King".

The Body of Christ. Amen.

"Not without reason do you say 'Amen', for you acknowledge in your heart that you are receiving the body of Christ. When you present yourself, the priest says to you, 'the body of Christ', and you reply 'Amen' that is, 'it is so'. Let the heart persevere in what the tongue confesses." (*Saint Ambrose*).

"Come to communion... It is true that you are not worthy of it, but you need it." (*The Curé d'Ars, Saint John Mary Vianney*).

The Concluding Rites

The Blessing and dismissal

"The love that we celebrate in the sacrament is not something we can keep to ourselves. By its very nature it demands to be shared with all. What the world needs is God's love; it needs to encounter Christ and to believe in him. The Eucharist is thus the source and summit not only of the Church's life, but also of her mission: 'an authentically Eucharistic Church is a missionary Church.' We too must tell our brothers and sisters with conviction: 'That which we have seen and heard we proclaim also to you, so that you may have fellowship with us'. Truly, nothing is more beautiful than to know Christ and to make him known to others." (*Pope Benedict XVI*).

Go in peace, glorifying the Lord by your life

"Receiving the Bread of Life, the disciples of Christ ready themselves to undertake with the strength of the Risen Lord and his Spirit the tasks which await them in their ordinary life. For the faithful who have understood the meaning of what they have done, the Eucharistic celebration does not stop at the church door. Like the first witnesses of the Resurrection, Christians who gather each Sunday to experience and proclaim the presence of the

Risen Lord are called to evangelize and bear witness in their daily lives. Given this, the Prayer after Communion and the Concluding Rite - the Final Blessing and the Dismissal - need to be better valued and appreciated, so that all who have shared in the Eucharist may come to a deeper sense of the responsibility which is entrusted to them. Once the assembly disperses, Christ's disciples return to their everyday surroundings with the commitment to make their whole life a gift, a spiritual sacrifice pleasing to God. They feel indebted to their brothers and sisters because of what they have received in the celebration, not unlike the disciples of Emmaus who, once they had recognized the Risen Christ 'in the breaking of the bread' felt the need to return immediately to share with their brothers and sisters the joy of meeting the Lord." (*Blessed Pope John Paul II*).

The Priest venerates the altar with a kiss. After making a profound bow with the ministers, he withdraws.

Conclusion

Nothing can replace reading, meditating and praying the texts of the liturgy. May this simple guide help the reader to enter more deeply into the celebration of the Mystery of Faith.

Participating in the Mass

Celebrating the liturgy with dignity and beauty

Abbot Cuthbert Johnson OSB, in this companion to his widely acclaimed CTS booklet "Understanding the Roman Missal", provides an informative, step-by-step, guide to the celebration of the Mass, to enable the Liturgy to be celebrated with reverence, dignity and beauty.

Abbot Cuthbert writes: "Every member of the worshiping community present at Mass has the responsibility of participating in the Liturgy in such a way as to contribute to the splendour of Divine Worship for the glory and praise of God."

Abbot Cuthbert Johnson, a Benedictine monk, liturgist and accomplished musician, is a Consultor to the Congregation for Divine Worship and an Advisor to the Vox Clara Committee.

ISBN: 978 1 86082 758 7

CTS Code: LT 03

Understanding the Roman Missal

A presentation and explanation of the
new translation, accompanied by liturgical
and spiritual reflections

The Church, not only in Britain but throughout the
whole English-speaking world, now has a new edition of
the Roman Missal. This booklet presents and explains the
new translation, together with a series of liturgical and
spiritual reflections.

Abbot Cuthbert Johnson, a Benedictine monk, liturgist and
accomplished musician, is a Consultor to the Congregation for
Divine Worship and an Advisor to the Vox Clara Committee.

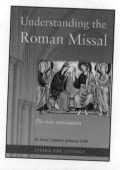

ISBN: 978 1 86082 737 2

CTS Code: LT 02